ALSO BY THE AUTHOR

From Lectern to Laboratory: How Science
and Technology Changed the Face
of America's Colleges

Circles, Lines, and Squiggles:
Astrology for the Curious-Minded

The Men Who Made the Yankees:
The Odyssey of the World's Greatest
Baseball Team from Baltimore to the Bronx

How We Are Smart: A Multicultural Approach
to the Theory of Multiple Intelligences

Dear Frank: Babe Ruth, the Red Sox,
and the Great War

The Things He Could Have Been

Stories of Babe Ruth

W. Nikola-Lisa

Copyright © 2023 by W. Nikola-Lisa
Published by Gyroscope Books, Chicago

Disclaimer: No part of this publication may be reproduced or transmitted in any form or by any means, electronic or mechanical, including mimeographing, recording, taping, scanning, via internet download, or by any information storage retrieval systems, without permission from the author, except by a reviewer who may quote passages in a review. For information about permissions to reproduce selections from this book, email the author at nikolabooks@gmail.com.

Ordering Information: For orders by US trade bookstores, retail outlets, and public libraries, contact the Ingram Content Group: Tel: Retail (800) 937-8000; Libraries (800) 937-5300; or visit www.ingramcontent.com

Publisher's Cataloging-In-Publication
(Provided by Cassidy Cataloguing Services, Inc,)

Names: Nikola-Lisa, W., author.
Title: The things he could have been : stories of Babe Ruth / W. Nikola-Lisa.
Description: [Chicago, Illinois] : Gyroscope Books, [2023] | Includes bibliographical references.
Identifiers: ISBN: 979-89860173-1-0 (paperback) | 979-89860173-2-7 (kindle)

Subjects: LCSH: Ruth, Babe, 1895-1948. | Baseball players--United States--Biography. | LCGFT: Biographies. | BISAC: YOUNG ADULT NONFICTION / Sports & Recreation / Baseball & Softball. | YOUNG ADULT NONFICTION / Biography & Autobiography / Sports & Recreation. | YOUNG ADULT NONFICTION / History / United States / 20th Century.

Classification: LCC: GV865.R8 N55 2023 | DDC: 796.357092--dc23

To George Herman "Babe" Ruth,
who started it all by walloping
an unthinkable 60 home runs in 1927

To Roger Eugene Maris, who clobbered
61 home runs for the Yankees
thirty-four years later

To Aaron James Judge,
who topped both Ruth and Maris
when he blasted 63 homers in 2022 to set
a new single-season home-run
record for the indomitable
Bronx Bombers

With special thanks to
Michael Reed
and Tom Greensfelder

Babe Ruth?

Why, everyone knows who
    Babe Ruth was—
Your mama knows.
Your papa knows.
Your aunts and uncles know.
Your cousins know.

Heck, your whole family knows who Babe Ruth was. But that doesn't mean they know all the things . . .

he could have been.

He could have been a . . .

JAZZ MAN

a real razz-ma-tazz man,

a foot-stompin' rag man.

Yes, he could have been—

but he wasn't.

BABE RUTH LOVED music. He loved it because he always had it around him in one way or another. His first, and perhaps best, instrument was his voice: it was deep and resonant, surprisingly so, and Ruth was not adverse to showing it off, which occasionally got him into trouble.

In the summer of 1920, his first year with the Yankees, Ruth was driving back from a game in Washington, DC, with his wife and several Yankee teammates. It was two in the morning. Ruth was at the wheel, singing at the top of his lungs (and driving much too fast for the winding country road). Just outside the hamlet of Wawa, southwest of Philadelphia, Ruth lost control of the big four-door touring car, flipping it over. Fortunately, Ruth and his companions walked away from the mishap with only minor scratches, but newspapers had a field day proclaiming "Ruth Reported Killed in Car Crash."

If he wasn't singing, Ruth was usually cranking up his portable phonograph, which he took with him on most road trips (along with his collection of 78-rpm records that he kept in his wife's cake tins for safekeeping). Many an evening was spent in Ruth's hotel room where there was always an abundance of people, from teammates to hangers-on, enjoying the good life. Curiously, Ruth often sat off to the side, surrounded by a cadre of admirers, like a king in his court, feeding his phonograph a steady diet of records.

Ruth was not adverse to pulling out his wind-up phonograph in the most unusual circumstances. For instance, during a barnstorming tour in the fall of 1926, Ruth held a "barn dance" beside a water tank when his train stopped to take on water in rural Montana. With one hand on the phonograph's handle and the other waving to the growing crowd of townspeople, Ruth beseeched them to sing and dance—which they did, much to Ruth's delight.

The Sultan of Swat was also known to pick up an instrument or two—saxophone, ukulele, tuba, whatever was within reach. But, no, you couldn't say that he was musically inclined. There's evidence of this in a photo taken of Ruth and teammate Lou Gehrig. While Ruth, eyes bulging and cheeks distended, tries to eke out a note on a saxophone, Gehrig, sitting nearby, plugs his ears with his index fingers. Of course, it's a promotional stunt because the same scene is replayed at Artie McGovern's gym several years later. While Ruth struggles to play a saxophone, two gym members grimace on either side of him, one the great band leader John Philip Sousa. Ruth certainly didn't have the chops to play music; but then again, his life was one long improvisation, an appropriate metaphor for the ginned-up jazz era in which he lived.

Of all the stories I found fascinating was one that had to do with a shotgun, a cat, and a piano. The scene takes place at Ruth's farm in Sudbury, Massachusetts, a large multi-acre plot of land that Ruth bought in 1922, naming it "Home Plate Farm." With the farm's resident cat curled up next to a piano in the front room, Ruth would quietly slide open a nearby window, out of which he would discharge a shotgun. The sudden blast would send Ruth's feline friend straight up into the air, only to land, claws outstretched, on top of a heavily scratched piano.

He could have been a . . .

RING MAN

an upper-cuttin' sting man,

a hook-'em-in-the-chin man.

Yes, he could have been—

but he wasn't.

BABE RUTH LEARNED to play baseball at St. Mary's Industrial School for Boys, an orphanage for wayward youth on the outskirts of Baltimore run by brothers of the Xaverian order. Although baseball was the preferred sport at St. Mary's, the boys (or "inmates," as they often referred to themselves) also played football, soccer, handball, volleyball, and basketball. They also held boxing and wrestling matches. Although baseball was Ruth's first love, boxing—and later golf—came in a close second. It was a sign of the times. Along with baseball, which was fast becoming the national pastime, boxing was a popular early twentieth-century sport.

Boxing wasn't for everyone, however. It was a blood sport, much too violent to supersede baseball as the national pastime. That didn't stop Ruth from threatening to become a professional boxer, especially when contract negotiations with Red Sox owner Harry Frazee stalled, as they often did. After the 1918 war-shortened season, in which Ruth claimed the home run title with 11 wallops, Ruth threatened to turn boxer if Frazee didn't raise his salary from $7,500 a year to $15,000.

Ruth let it be known that he had an offer to fight Edward "Gunboat" Smith, a heavyweight boxer of Irish-American descent, if Frazee didn't meet his salary demands. The two danced around each other until they finally settled on a three-year contract at $10,000 a year. And why wouldn't they: the truth is Frazee needed Ruth as much as Ruth needed Frazee.

It wasn't until Ruth joined Artie McGovern's gym in midtown Manhattan after a disastrous 1925 season that Ruth got a close-up view of the boxing world, but not as blood sport, rather as an effective way to train during the off-season. A former flyweight boxer, McGovern grew up in Hell's Kitchen, a tough West Side neighborhood. He was a small man who never sat still, a dynamo who ran a gymnasium on the fourth floor of the Liggett Building located at the corner of 42nd Street and Madison Avenue. He was more than a trainer though: he was a health nut who became a national authority on physical fitness, selling the McGovern Method of Physical Reconstruction to the rich and famous.

McGovern's budding enterprise was part of a larger health craze sweeping the country. McGovern took Ruth under his wing in 1925 after Ruth came down with what the press referred to as "The Bellyache Heard Round the World." Ruth was a physical wreck when he showed up at McGovern's gym around the middle of December, weighing in at 254 pounds, up from his usual 220. According to McGovern, Ruth's blood pressure was low, his pulse was high, his stomach bloated, and his muscles soft and flabby.

In any case, McGovern saw his work cut out for him—and so did Ruth, who threw himself wholeheartedly into McGovern's program. After spending the winter working out at the gym—lifting weights, jumping rope, working the punching bag, and occasionally stepping into the ring to spar with an opponent—Ruth showed up at spring training before the 1926 season having shed more than forty pounds. The result: The Titan of Terror had one of the best seasons of his career.

He could have been a . . .

CATTLE MAN

a bronco-bustin' saddle man,

a rough-ridin' range man.

Yes, he could have been—

but he wasn't.

THERE'S A GREAT image of Babe Ruth and Lou Gehrig, Ruth's teammate, at Dexter Park in Brooklyn, New York, in 1927, at the beginning of a post-season barnstorming tour after the Yankees won the 1927 World Series. Ruth is shown sitting astride the hood of an automobile outfitted with the gently curving horns of a longhorn steer. Decked out in full cowboy regalia, replete with lasso and ten-gallon hat, Ruth and Gehrig wave their hats at the crowd. All eyes are on the famous duo, but especially on Ruth who broke the single-season home-run record that year with 60 out-of-the-park wallops.

But could the Sultan of Swat hit it out of the ball park as a rancher? It's possible. As I mentioned earlier, he owned a farm, a large multi-acre tract in

Sudbury, Massachusetts, 30 miles west of Boston. During the off-season, Ruth would often retreat to his farm where he would hunt, fish, clear trees, and chop wood; that is, when he wasn't running off to New York City to have some fun in his specially equipped limousine (what made it special: the 55-gallon gas tank that Ruth had installed so he wouldn't have to stop for gas on the way).

The latter anecdote just might be the answer to the question posed above: it was Ruth's perennial running off to have some fun that would probably disqualify him from being a successful rancher. For instance, after his favorite English bull terrier got loose and killed a neighbor's pedigreed cow in the fall of 1925, an unfortunate rampage that set him back several thousand dollars, Ruth told reporters that he hated farming, hated Home Plate Farm, and was planning to sell and move to Florida (which might not have been a bad idea given his dismal performance in 1925, a season that ended abruptly with a trip to the hospital with an undiagnosed intestinal disorder).

Although he bought Home Plate Farm in 1922, Ruth was not unfamiliar with the surrounding area, having stayed in and around Sudbury while playing for the Boston Red Sox, his first major league team. Like other Red Sox players, Ruth rented a cottage during the off-season, enjoying all that the rural environment had to offer (for a city kid from a strictly run orphanage, this was quite a thrill). One of the first places Ruth rented was a one-room cottage that Ruth fondly named "Ihatetoquitit" cottage. The twenty-by-fifty-foot room featured fold-down cots, a Franklin stove, a string of Japanese lanterns, an upright piano, and an assortment of flags from around the world (except Germany due to the recency of the First World War).

By 1922, Ruth, now playing for the New York Yankees, was one of the highest paid baseball players in the major leagues: he could afford to buy a second—or third, or fourth—house, and he did, purchasing one of the oldest homes (and largest, with twelve rooms) in the area. Along with the house, there was a barn, a garage (which supposedly could accommodate four horses and twelve cars), and a henhouse around back. But a rancher? A successful cattleman? I doubt it. Ruth was a baseball player: it's as simple as that.

He could have been a . . .

SCREEN MAN

a leading-lady's dream man,

a don't-forget-your-lines man.

Yes, he could have been—

but he wasn't.

A MOVIE STAR? Babe Ruth? Nonsense. Everyone knows that Babe Ruth was a baseball player, the greatest baseball player of his time, perhaps of all time. But then, it was the 1920s when syndicated newspapers, sports weeklies, radio broadcasts, newsreels, and movies were beginning to knit the country together into one mass communication whole. In other words, the setting was ripe for the oversized personality of George Herman "Babe" Ruth to take the nation by storm. And he did, with the help of Christy Walsh, his business manager, through barnstorming tours, vaudeville acts, product endorsements, radio broadcasts, and, yes, movie appearances.

Ruth's big break came in 1920 during his first year with the Yankees. Midway through the season, after he hit his 30th home run, one more than he did the entire year before, Ruth received an offer to make a movie about a small town simpleton who rises to baseball stardom. Although the movie, a black-and-white silent film called *Headin' Home*, was a box office flop, the national exposure helped fuel Ruth's rise to stardom. Over the next two decades, right up to his death in 1948, Ruth would appear in almost a dozen movies, from instructional shorts to full-length feature films.

After *Headin' Home*, Ruth starred in *Babe Comes Home*, which was shot in Los Angeles before the 1927 season. The Bambino plays "Babe Dugan," the star of his baseball team, who has the irritating habit of splattering chewing tobacco all over his uniform. After the team cleaners call in Vernie, their best laundress, Dugan and the laundress fall in love. You can guess the ending: after they have falling-out, Dugan, encouraged by Vernie, slugs the winning home run of an important game, whereby Dugan swears off tobacco and the couple happily reunite. Predictable? Yes. But also highly successful (supposedly earning more money for Ruth than his entire year's baseball salary, which was a nifty $52,000 or, as Ruth had wanted, a grand a week).

The next film of note that Ruth appeared in was a 1942 biopic of teammate Lou Gehrig, who died the year before the film was released of amyotrophic lateral sclerosis (ALS), known today as Lou Gehrig's disease. Starring Gary Cooper as Lou Gehrig, *The Pride of the Yankees* is less sports biography and more a tribute to the legendary New York Yankee first baseman. The film is populated by several of Gehrig's teammates playing themselves, including Bob Meusel, Mark Koenig, Bill Dickey, and, yes, the incorrigible Babe Ruth, who by 1942 was out of shape and grossly overweight, motivating the Behemoth of Bust to shed 47 pounds in 60 days, a feat that landed him in the hospital for a brief, but dramatic, stay.

The last film made during Ruth's lifetime was *The Babe Ruth Story*, based on a book by the same name by sportswriter Bob Considine. Ruth, too old and too sick to play himself, was hired as a technical advisor to teach the film's star, William Bendix, how to swing a bat for the fences (although, truthfully, Ruth's real job was front man; that is, public relations). Like *Headin' Home*, the film bombed, and Ruth—his body ravaged with cancer—died a month later.

He could have been a . . .

LINKS MAN

a big-ol'-grin-and-winks man,

a hit-'em-straight-and-true man.

Yes, he could have been—

   but he wasn't.

BABE RUTH PLAYED golf, but then so did many other baseball players. There were two good reasons for this. First of all, it was excellent outdoor exercise, a perfect complement to spring training fitness sessions. After the Philadelphia Athletics incorporated golf into their spring training camps in 1910, other major league teams encouraged players to take up the game.

The second reason baseball players took up golf is that in the early twentieth century teams often traveled by train, a much slower form of transportation than today's chartered jet. As a consequence, players often had a lot of time on their hands, so off they headed to the nearest golf course.

That's how Ruth came to golf. Midway through the 1914 season, Jack Dunn, the owner of the minor league Baltimore Orioles, sold Ruth and two other players to the Boston Red Sox. Dunn needed the money and Ruth needed a bigger stage. It was a good move, both in terms of Ruth's baseball career and also his exposure to the game of golf. Many Red Sox players enjoyed a round or two of golf while waiting for the opposing team to arrive. Soon, Ruth was tagging along.

Although he was a natural baseball player, you couldn't say that Babe Ruth was a natural golfer. But he continued to play, and thanks to years of private lessons he improved steadily, and this despite the fact that several pros believed he had two strikes against him: he was left-handed (a taboo in the right-handed world of golf) and he swung at a golf ball the same way he swung at a baseball—with everything he had.

Regarding the former, Ruth considered playing right-handed, believing, as those who supported the "conversion" theory did, that his natural left-handedness would give him more control of the backswing and more power on the forward swing. But he never converted: he was just too comfortable with his left-handed stance.

Regarding the latter, although it cost him some accuracy on the fairways, it was Ruth's powerful baseball swing that was a perfect match for the golf course. As one golf pro at the time noted, Ruth's baseball swing and his golf swing were really one-and-the-same, just executed at different angles.

Given Ruth's love of golf, his competitive spirit, and his consistent single-digit handicap, did the Sultan of Swat ever consider turning pro? It's an interesting question. Then again, why would the greatest baseball player of his time turn professional golfer? And yet, at the end of his career, Ruth seriously considered turning pro. As an amateur, he was a top-flight player. But there's a difference between a top-flight amateur and a professional, and Ruth just didn't have what it took to be a professional.

First of all, he hardly broke par, maybe once or twice. But what really doomed him is something that golf great Walter Hagen observed: he lacked concentration, especially after the 10th hole (which, coincidently, took about the same time to play as a nine-inning baseball game).

In other words, his bluster about turning pro, which he often threatened, was just that: yes, he was a good golfer, one who raised the esteem of the game in the eyes of the public. But a pro? I don't think so, and neither did Ruth.

He could have been a . . .

FLASH MAN

a take-your-mug-for-cash man,

a camera-totin' press man.

Yes, he could have been—

but he wasn't.

THE GREAT BAMBINO was the darling of photographers, not only was Ruth a willing subject, but also his face had unique photogenic qualities. Marshall Hunt of the *New York Daily News* summed up those qualities this way: "The Speed Graphic, the newspaper photographer's camera of choice, loved his broad face with its flat nose and tiny eyes, loved his absolutely unique look, features put together in a hurry, an out-of-focus bulldog, no veneer or sanding involved."

It was an instantly recognizable face. The reason: Ruth's baseball career coincided with the Golden Age of Newspapering. During this era, two things fueled Ruth's rising stardom: the transformation of the newspaper's back page into the "front page" of the sports section and the replacement of the hand-drawn illustration with the realism of the still photograph. Ruth's manager understood the importance of this.

Throughout his career, Christy Walsh made it a habit to get Ruth in front of every camera he could. Ruth obliged, gladly, posing with movie stars, politicians, foreign royalty, children from all walks of life, as well as a host of animals (a chimpanzee, a tortoise, a prize-winning hen, and, for National Lobster Day, a beet-red lobster, to name a few). It was both Ruth's willingness to stand in front of a camera and his unique photogenic qualities that made him the darling of newspaper photographers.

But what about Ruth's photographic eye? We know he had a camera and delighted in filling family photo albums. But did he have the eye of a professional photographer? Looking at Ruth's family albums you'd probably say no, certainly not in the way that professional photographers have. But Ruth did have an eye—an eye for hitting a baseball. He must have. He clobbered 714 home runs in his 22-year career, almost twice as many as the next career home-run leader. Yes, Ruth had a talent for hitting.

But where did it come from? The whole world wanted to know, so in 1921 Christy Walsh enlisted the help of scientists at Columbia University, where they ran a battery of tests on the Caliph of Clout to gauge his eyesight, motor skills, and cognitive performance. Although the testing procedures were primitive compared to today's high-tech analyses, the results were undeniable: Ruth was superhuman, with an almost perfect coordination of eyes, brain, nerves, and muscle, 20-30 percent better than the average prson. His eyesight, in particular, caught researchers' attention: whereas the average person responded to light stimulus in 0.180 of a second, Ruth needed only 0.160 of a second. In baseball terms that meant a pitcher had to throw a baseball twenty-thousandths (0.020) of a second faster to strike Ruth out than to strike out the average batter.

So, did Ruth have a photographer's eye? Given the photographs in his family albums, probably not. What he had was a slugger's eye that gave him the uncanny ability to "see the ball," enabling him to smack it out of the ballpark more often than any other player of his time.

He could have been a . . .

PAD MAN

a shoulder-blockin' bad man,

a hit-'em-where-it-hurts man.

Yes, he could have been—

but he wasn't.

BY THE EARLY decades of the twentieth century American football was beginning to catch on. Though the organization of the sport lagged several decades behind baseball, professional football as a money-making enterprise was around the corner, something Ruth's manager understood.

In 1924, with his sports management company thriving, Christy Walsh established the "All American Board of Football," which recruited college football coaches to ghost write articles analyzing football games and other related events. One of Walsh's greatest recruits, however, wasn't a college football coach, but the hard-hitting Yankee slugger Babe Ruth, who often appeared on the gridiron during the off-season.

Take the 1926 post-season barnstorming tour when Ruth and several teammates headed west after losing the

World Series to the St. Louis Cardinals. After threading their way through a string of small Midwestern towns, they arrived in Minneapolis in early November for an unexpected stop at the University of Minnesota to watch the school's football team practice. After entertaining the team with his baseball exploits, Ruth donned football pads and took to the field, taking a few snaps with the offensive line, after which he waved a hearty good-bye to the squad and disappeared into the cold November air.

Several weeks later, Ruth did the same while visiting Drake University in Des Moines, Iowa, at the invitation of head coach Ossie Solem. After the Colossus of Clout showed off his passing and punting skills, Ruth scrimmaged with the varsity squad, first knocking the team's star fullback to the ground and, later, scoring a 20-yard touchdown.

Several photographs exist showing Ruth suited up in pads, looking at ease on the gridiron. But as everyone knows it's a ploy, a staged promotional event. Nonetheless, he was there in full football regalia, there to entertain, to make people laugh, and all for the benefit of the local press.

Walsh was a genius at keeping Ruth in the newspapers. He had the Titan of Terror splashed across the sports pages on a regular basis. But shots of Ruth suited up in football attire were not always taken on the gridiron, as Ruth's appearance at the Palmer House in Chicago on November 25, 1927, demonstrates. Ruth and teammate Lou Gehrig showed up in pads at a pre-game banquet the night before Notre Dame squared off against the University of Southern California in Chicago's Soldier Field.

Although Ruth could play baseball like a fullback, did he have it in him to play professional football? Throughout his career, especially when negotiating a new contract, Ruth often threatened to become a boxer, or a golfer, even a movie star. But he never once threatened to play professional football. Perhaps deep down Ruth knew he wasn't cut out to play the game. More than that, it's what Ruth believed about baseball. Speaking at Yankee Stadium on "Babe Ruth Day" on Sunday, April 27, 1947, the year before the Yankees retired his uniform, Ruth said it himself: "The only real game in the world, I think, is baseball."

For once, the Sultan of Swat, the Titan of Terror, the Wizard of Whack, the Prince of Pounders, the Big Bam wasn't joking.

He could have been a . . .

FIREMAN

a climb-the-ladder-higher man,

a death-defying rescue man.

Yes, he could have been—

but he wasn't.

NO DOUBT ABOUT it: Babe Ruth was a ham, a show-off, a larger-than-life personality who dominated any social situation in which he was thrust. To many, he was an overgrown child—a "man-child"—who loved to clown around. The lines "He could have been a fireman, a climb-the-ladder-higher man..." were inspired by a photograph I stumbled upon while researching this book. The photograph is dated 1928.

It's early in the season, but late in Ruth's career, and the Bambino is sporting a fireman's jacket and matching helmet. The location is Comiskey Park on Chicago's south side, home of the American League's Chicago White Sox. Although the gear fits him well, the Yankee slugger seems uneasy, out of place, even with his slightly roguish smile. Perhaps it's the way he holds the fireman's ax—like a baseball bat. On the other hand, Ruth was certainly strong enough to be a fireman, and he had a certain fearless, if not reckless, quality about him to be good at it. So, maybe, it's not that far-fetched to believe that the King of Crash could have been a fireman; but of course we know he wasn't.

Fire did burst into Ruth's life on two separate occasions, however. The first incident occurred during the 1919 season when Ruth received word that his alma mater, St. Mary's Industrial School for Boys, had suffered a devastating fire that destroyed the main administrative building and a dormitory completed only ten years earlier. Fortunately, St. Mary's Chapel, at the corner of Wilkins and Caton Avenues, sustained only smoke and water damage.

As he did so many times during his career, Ruth reached out, arranging for members of the school band to travel with the Yankees at the end of the 1920 season. Wherever the Yankees played, Ruth helped the band stage concerts in order to raise money for the school's rebuilding efforts. Ruth posed for dozens of photographs with members of the band, often wearing a sailor's cap and holding a tuba. But what the boys remember the most—and there were certainly lots of memories—was Ruth supplying them with unlimited quantities of ice cream on the train while riding to their next destination.

The second time fire touched Ruth's life was a much sadder occasion. On January 11, 1929, ten years after the St. Mary's fire, and three years after Ruth and his first wife, Helen Woodford, separated, a fire swept through a six-room cottage in Watertown, Massachusetts, that Edward Kinder, a local dentist, and Ruth's ex-wife Helen shared. With Kinder at Boston Garden, where he frequently went to watch the Friday night fights, Helen retired to her bedroom upstairs. Sometime around midnight the house caught fire, allegedly due to faulty electrical wiring. By the time the fire department arrived, Helen was lying on her bedroom floor near the door, unconscious. She died hours later.

Kinder was distraught. Ruth devastated. The press pounced: Was it really an accident? And just who was Edward Kinder? Ultimately, detectives concluded that the fire was an accident. Helen was buried, Kinder disappeared, and Ruth, after pleading with the press to let his wife die in peace, went back to doing what he did best—slugging baseballs over the outfield wall.

He could have been a . . .

HALL MAN

a cue-stick-and-a-ball man,

a rack-'em-up-again man.

Yes, he could have been—

but he wasn't.

I'M HOLDING A photograph of Babe Ruth bending his top-heavy 6'2", 220-pound frame over the edge of a pool table. I could be looking at Jackie Gleason playing Minnesota Fats in the 1961 motion picture *The Hustler*, but I'm not. I'm looking at the Colossus of Clout posing for a crowd of bemused onlookers. Ruth liked sports, all kinds of sports, but especially sports that you could bet on. As a player he couldn't bet on baseball, so he did the next best thing: he bet on horse races, card games, golf matches, pool games, you name it.

Why all the betting? Perhaps it was just too much time on his hands, or too much money in his pockets. On the other hand, he could have inherited the interest from Frank Ferrell, one of the first owners of the American League's Hilltop Highlanders (a decade later we would know them as the New York Yankees). Ferrell was known as New York City's Poolroom King, a tip of the hat to his domination of the gambling hall. His Hilltop Highlander co-owner was "Big Bill" Devery, an ex-police commissioner indicted for, but never convicted of, corruption. The duo bought the minor league Baltimore Orioles in 1903 from American League president Ban Johnson for $18,000, promptly moving the team to upper Manhattan where it played in American League Park (otherwise known as Hilltop Park as the ballpark sat on a high point in the Washington Heights neighborhood).

It was a gamble. In Manhattan, the National League's New York Giants dominated major league baseball, having recruited John "Mugsy" McGraw, the scrappy player/manager of the old major league Baltimore Orioles, the National League's most dominant team. After more than a decade of low attendance and mounting debt, Ferrell and Devery sold the Highlanders to two millionaires, Col. Jake Ruppert and Tillinghast L'Hommedieu "Cap" Huston, who in just a few short years would make the purchase of the century, acquiring George Herman "Babe" Ruth from the Boston Red Sox. And, as they say, the rest is history.

As for pool (or billiards, the game's traditional name), Ruth played, or at least we assume that he did. After Ruth married Claire Hodgson in 1929, the Sultan of Swat showed off the newlyweds' 11-room apartment on West 88th Street, which included a billiard room, even though no billiard table had been installed. So, yes, Ruth played, but he didn't play seriously, that is, for money. He'd already been hustled on the golf course by Sammy Byrd, his New York Yankee teammate. So, no, he wasn't a pool shark, a hustler, willing to risk serious money (the way he did early in his career on a trip to Havana in 1919, when he lost almost a year's salary to local hustlers).

But there is a connection between Ruth and the game of billiards. When Ruth connected with a baseball, sending it high over the outfield wall, there was that recognizable sound, that "click" of bat on ball, similar to the sound that two billiard balls make when they collide. Only in Ruth's case, in the world of major league baseball, the Titan of Terror sent the little white pellet much, much farther than he could any billiard ball.

He could have been a . . .

LAW MAN

a beat-'em-to-the-draw man,

a keep-the-peace-and-calm man.

Yes, he could have been—

but he wasn't.

BABE RUTH HAD a healthy respect for the police, but usually only after he had been caught breaking the law. His contact with police began early, as a youth growing up in the rough-and-tumble Baltimore waterfront where, at age seven, after being deemed "incorrigible," he was shunted off to St. Mary's Industrial School for Boys.

Some say he took the Wilkins Avenue bus to St. Mary's with is father, George, Sr. Others say he was escorted by the local beat patrolman who was familiar with the family. In either case, Ruth spent the greater part of his youth at St. Mary's under the tutelage of the brothers of the Xaverian Order who ran the institution. Was it the stern, disciplined approach they took to residents of St. Mary's that began Ruth's healthy respect for authority? Perhaps.

Whatever the cause, it didn't curtail Ruth from misbehaving, even as an adult.

As a member of the New York Yankees he was often caught speeding up Riverside Drive in his super-charged 12-cylinder roadster on his way to an afternoon game. Usually Ruth was given a warning, occasionally a fine, but in early June of 1921, the traffic cop took Ruth before a local judge who threw Ruth in the slammer (the Big Bam had already made a couple of appearances before the magistrate earlier that month).

With reporters hovering outside the police station (one perched atop a building across the street hoping to get a photo of the Sultan of Swat in his cell), Ruth was released a few minutes before 4:00 p.m. With his uniform donned beneath his street clothes (Ruth had the foresight to use his only phone call to have a Yankee trainer bring his uniform to the station), Ruth was hustled to a side door where he jumped into his waiting roadster and, with the help of a police escort, flew to the Polo Grounds where the Yankees played their home games, arriving just in time for the sixth inning of a game between the Yankees and the Cleveland Indians and, as word spread of his release, to a standing ovation for his not-quite-on-time plate appearance.

But let there be no mistake about it: Babe Ruth didn't have an adversarial relationship with the police. Quite the contrary, as he often relied on them for protection, especially when fans swarmed onto the field before the end of a game, which they often did in the late innings after Ruth slugged another one of his towering, jaw-dropping home runs. In one instance, he clung desperately to the tail of a mounted policeman's horse in order to be pulled through the crowd. In relying on the police, Ruth often gave back: he attended police banquets; he helped with police fundraising events; he even became an honorary member of the New York City Police Reserves, where he was assigned—where else?—to the "recreation" department.

Even in death, Ruth relied on the police. When his body laid in state at Yankee Stadium, a police honor guard watched over it as more than seventy-seven thousand mourners filed by to pay their respects. But a policeman? No, Ruth was too much of a "bad boy," an irreverent derring-do and man-about-town, which meant his uniform would always be pinstriped, never solid blue.

Yes, Babe Ruth could have been many things:

a jazz man, a ring man,

a cattle man, a links man.

But he wasn't.

And why wasn't he?

'Cause he was the Babe, that's why—
George Herman "Babe" Ruth, the hard-hittin' homerun king of the world champion New York Yankees.

A giant in his time.

TO MANY, ESPECIALLY children, Babe Ruth was a giant—literally—a powerfully built man who stood over six feet tall, a change from the slim, scrappy player of the "nickel-and-dime" era whose job it was to get on base by any means possible. Ruth's size and brawn changed that: he swung for the fences every time he stepped into the batter's box, often corkscrewing himself into the ground when he missed.

Enter the "live ball" era, the age of the long ball. What better way to draw fans to the ballpark than with the hope of seeing one of Ruth's towering home runs. Ruth said it himself: "The fans would rather see me hit one homer to right than three doubles to left."

But Ruth didn't begin his major league career as a slugger (although there were intimations of that early in his career). He began in 1914 as one of the

American League's best left-handed pitchers, taking the mound for Harry Frazee's Boston Red Sox, helping the franchise win three world championship titles in the five-and-a-half years he played for it. Technically, you could argue four championship titles, if you count the title he helped the Providence Grays, Frazee's minor league team, win in 1914.

Yes, Ruth was a giant, especially on the mound early in his career. In 1915, after breaking into the pitching rotation mid-season, Ruth went 18-8 with a 2.44 ERA. The next year he did even better, with a 23-12 record and a league-leading 1.75 ERA, five of those wins against the great Walter Johnson of the Washington Senators. In 1917, Ruth continued his pitching prowess, ending the season with a 24-13 record and a 2.01 ERA. Just as notable, Ruth completed 35 of the 38 games he started (although it should be noted that during Ruth's era it was not unusual for pitchers to pitch an entire game, sometimes both games of a double-header).

The 1918 season was a pivot point for Ruth. Although his pitching record was a solid 13-7 during the war-shortened season, he began to perform just as well at the plate, winning his first of many home-run titles with 11 dingers, a title he shared with Tilly Walker of the Philadelphia Athletics.

Fans were not the only ones who noticed, Ruppert and Huston did as well. But before the co-owners of the Yankees acquired him at the end of the 1919 season, Ruth logged in one more pitching record: he pitched 29.7 scoreless innings during his World Series appearances with the Boston Red Sox, a record that stood until 1961 when another left-handed Yankee pitcher, Whitey Ford, broke it.

The 1920 season saw Ruth in a new uniform—the snappy blue pinstripes of the New York Yankees. In the lineup almost everyday as a regular in the outfield, now Ruth could concentrate on what he loved doing the most—swinging a baseball bat. In his 15 years that he swung a bat for the New York Yankees, the Great Bambino helped the Yankees win seven American League pennants and four World Series championships. And he did it mostly with his bat, earning him a number of sobriquets: The Sultan of Swat, The Titan of Terror, The Colossus of Clout, The Behemoth of Bust, The Wizard of Wham, The Maharaja of Mash, The Prince of Pounders, to name just a few.

In 1920, his first year with the Yankees, Ruth averaged .376 at the plate, batted in 137 runs, and slugged a whopping 54 home runs (almost double his output the year before in his last season with the Red Sox). In 1921, Ruth's batting average climbed to .378, the highest mark he would achieve in a single season. He also drove in 171 runs and clobbered 59 home runs, his third of four record-setting seasons. In 1922, Ruth's output slowed a bit: he batted .315, drove in 99 runs, and walloped a mere 35 home runs.

He would improve on those stats over the next five years, except for the 1925 season when an intestinal disorder took him out of the lineup for the first two months of the season. Ruth's barrage at the plate would culminate in his record-breaking 1927 season when he batted .356, drove in 164 runs, scored 158 runs, and sent 60 white pellets screaming over the outfield fences.

Ruth's statistics in a Yankee uniform are truly remarkable. His batting average was .300 or higher every year he played with the Yankees except 1925, the year he missed the first part of the season, and 1934, his last year with the Yankees. And he drove in 100 or more runs in 12 out of 15 years wearing Yankee pinstripes.

When it comes to home-run output, Ruth was head-and-shoulders above every other player of his era, setting the single-season home-run record four times during his 22-year career: once with the Boston Red Sox, slugging 29 home runs in 1919, and three times with the Yankees, where he almost doubled his output, walloping 54 home runs in 1920, 59 in 1921, and 60 in 1927, a record that would stand for 34 years until New York Yankee outfielder Roger Maris broke it in 1961, slugging 61 home runs that year.

Ruth's home-run record meant that he often led the American League in single-season home runs. With all of this in mind, it should come as no surprise that the Prince of Pounders was one of the first of five electees to be inducted into the newly-established Baseball Hall of Fame in Cooperstown, New York, in 1936.

Now, let's consider Babe Ruth's career stats against all other players who've played in the major leagues during the modern era, from 1900 to the present. Ruth is first in slugging percentage (.690), first in on-base plus slugging percentage (1.164), second in on-base percentage (.474), second in runs batted in (2,213), third in walks (2,062), third in home runs (714), fourth in runs scored (2,174), sixth in total bases (5,793), and, not to be overlooked, tenth in batting average (.342), batting over .350 eight times in his career.

In short, George Herman "Babe" Ruth was everything the press made him out to be. He was a baby-faced, crowd-pleasing giant of a man who sought the attention of those around him, as well as their approval, and he got it both on the field with his incomparable baseball skills and off the field with his irrepressible, larger-than-life personality.

CITATIONS

Ruth reported killed... The headline of a local newspaper that got wind of Ruth's almost fatal crash on a Pennsylvania back road. Creamer, Robert W. *Babe*, p. 231, loc. 1249.

The bellyache heard... According to Leigh Montville, it was W. O. McGeehan of the *New York Tribune* who coined the phrase "The Bellyache Heard Round the World" after Ruth landed in the hospital with an undiagnosed intestinal disorder during the 1925 season. Montville, Leigh. *The Big Bam*, p. 203, loc. 3812.

The Speed Graphic... The Speed Graphic was developed in 1912 by a camera manufacturing company in Rochester, New York, for commercial photography, especially for the emerging world of photojournalism. The name, however, is an oxymoron: the Speed Graphic was anything but fast, certainly not like the point-and-shoot cameras of today. Montville, Leigh. *The Big Bam*, p. 160, loc. 2975.

Number of sobriquets... Newspapers had a field day with Babe Ruth. Photographers loved his wide-eyed, full-moon baby face, as well as his what-do-you-want-me-to-do-next attitude. The press couldn't generate enough descriptive phrases to contain him. For a tongue-in-cheek look at some of these sobriquets, e.g., The Sultan of Swat, The Caliph of Clout, The Prince of Pounders, etc., I recommend Jane Leavy's *The Big Fella* where she reels off a host of titles, both real and imagined. Leavy, Jane. *The Big Fella*, p. 17, loc. 501.

Ruth was superhuman... The results of Columbia University's battery of tests on Ruth were reported in the October 1921 issue of *Popular Science Monthly*, a year after physicist A. L. Hodges published a syndicated newspaper article in the *Richmond Times-Dispatch* under the title, "Science Explains 'Babe' Ruth's Home Runs, Interesting Principles of Physics and Psychology Involved in the 44 Horse-Power Swing Which Shoots the Ball Skyward at Six Miles a Minute," wherein Hodges concludes that over the course of a fifty-home-run season, Ruth would expend enough energy to lift a fifty-five-ton locomotive six inches off the ground. Leavy, Jane. *The Big Fella*, pp. 303-305, loc. 4727-4749.

The only real... New York Yankee fans loved Babe Ruth, even after he left the Yankees with the promise of managing the American League's Boston Braves. Yankee management felt otherwise: the aging Ruth was a real pain in the neck, constantly lobbying to take over the helm of the Yankees after his playing days were over. It never happened, nor did it happen in Boston either. But Ruth, who loved the game of baseball, never gave up trying. Creamer, Robert W. *Babe*, p. 418, loc. 6087.

The fans would... This quotation can be found on the Baseball Hall of Fame's Babe Ruth page, along with several other witticisms, two of which go hand-in-hand. One by former teammate Joe Dugan, "To understand him you had to understand this: He wasn't human." The other by sportswriter Tommy Holmes, who quipped, "Some 20 years ago, I stopped talking about the Babe for the simple reason that I realized that those who had never seen him didn't believe me." Baseball Hall of Fame (https://baseballhall.org/hall-of-famers/ruth-babe), accessed 12-20-2022.

WORKS CONSULTED

Babe Ruth Birthplace and Museum, https://baberuthmuseum.org.

Baseball Hall of Fame, https://baseballhall.org.

Baseball Reference, https://www.baseball-reference.com.

Creamer, Robert W. *Babe: The Legend Comes to Life*. New York: Open Road Media, 2011. Kindle Edition.

Hampton, Wilborn. *Up Close: Babe Ruth, a Twentieth-Century Life*. New York: Viking, 2009. Penguin Young Readers Group. Kindle Edition.

Leavy, Jane. *The Big Fella: Babe Ruth and the World He Created*. New York: Harper, 2018. Kindle Edition.

Montville, Leigh. *The Big Bam: The Life and Times of Babe Ruth*. New York: Anchor, 2006. Kindle Edition.

Nowlin, Bill and Glen Sparks, et al (eds.). *The Babe*. Phoenix, AZ: Society for American Baseball Research, 2019. Society for American Baseball Research (SABR). Kindle Edition.

Society for American Baseball Research (SABR), https://sabr.org.

Vogel, Douglas. *Babe Ruth and the Scottish Game: Anecdotes of a Golf Fanatic*. Seattle: Chin Music Publishing, 2016. Kindle Edition.

IMAGE CREDITS

Attribution in order of appearance. All images have been desaturated, cropped, and modified using the "cut out" filter in Adobe Photoshop.

background baseballs... Shutterstock, cctm (2139740881)

ruth at bat... Alamy, RLPM Collection (2H8YA60)

jazz man... Shutterstock, Kiselev Valerevick (279124679)

ring man... Shutterstock, Everett Collection (484245040)

cattle man... Shutterstock, Janice Storch (420881644)

screen man... Shutterstock, Stokkete (239019985)

links man... Shutterstock, Everett Collection (242288590)

flash man... Shutterstock, Everett Collection (99830894)

pad man... Shutterstock, Everett Collection (314931521)

fireman... Shutterstock, Everett Collection (249572971)

hall man... Shutterstock, Everett Collection (100209392)

law man... Shutterstock, Everett Collection (227271562)

ruth waving hat... Alamy, Everett Collection (CWABRR)

ABOUT THE AUTHOR

W. Nikola-Lisa has been thinking about baseball ever since he played his first game of stickball as a youngster. Organized baseball followed, culminating in four years roaming the outfield for his high school varsity squad. The interest has lingered, resulting in two previous books about baseball: *The Men Who Made the Yankees: The Odyssey of the World's Greatest Baseball Team from Baltimore to the Bronx* and *Dear Frank: Babe Ruth, the Red Sox, and the Great War*. For more information about the author and his work, visit www.nikolabooks.com.